# Table of Contents

# Introduction

Dietary approach to stop hypertension has beneficial effects on NAFLD. This diet is rich in fruits, vegetables, whole grains, fish, poultry, nuts, legumes and low-fat dairy products; it has low levels of sodium, added sugars and fat. Finally, this diet emphasizes on the consumption fresh food.

Fatty liver disease (FLD), also known as hepatic steatosis, is a condition where excess fat builds up in the liver. Often there are no or few symptoms. Occasionally there may be tiredness or pain in the upper right side of the abdomen. Complications may include cirrhosis, liver cancer, and esophageal varices.

## History Of Fatty Liver

Alcoholic fatty liver is the earliest stage of alcohol-related liver disease. Heavy drinking damages the liver, and the liver can't break down fats as a result. Abstaining from alcohol will likely cause the fatty liver to subside. Within six weeks of not drinking alcohol, the fat can disappear.

## Epidemiology and Natural History of Non-alcoholic Fatty Liver Disease

Non-alcoholic fatty liver disease (NAFLD) is an important cause of liver disease burden across the world. By definition, although the histopathologic features of NAFLD are identical to that of alcoholic liver disease, its diagnosis requires absence of significant alcohol use and absence of other causes of chronic liver disease. We now know that NAFLD is not simply a disease of the Western world. It is manifested across the world, in varying rates, across gender, across varying ethnicities, and in its association with other host factors. In this review article, the definition of NAFLD, its spectrum, ranging from mild steatosis to hepatocellular injury and inflammation defined as non-alcoholic steatohepatitis (NASH) is discussed. Mild steatosis is generally a stable disease whereas NASH can be progressive. Based on current published literature, current incidence and prevalence of NAFLD and NASH are discussed. It is also accepted that these processes will continue to increase in prevalence with the rise of obesity, type II diabetes, and associated metabolic syndrome. Some of the risk factors have been well-established and are discussed. In addition, this review also presents emerging associations with other risk factors for NAFLD. Natural history of NAFLD is variable depending upon the histologic subtypes and other underlying comorbidities and is discussed in this review as well.

The liver, located on the upper-right side of the abdomen, is the largest internal organ of the human body. The main functions of the liver are to remove toxins and process food nutrients. Blood from the digestive system filters through the liver before travelling anywhere else in the body.

Fatty liver disease (steatosis) is the build-up of excess fat in the liver cells, and is a common liver complaint in Western countries. It affects about one in every 10 people. It is normal for the liver to contain some fat, but if fat accounts for more than 10 per cent of the liver's weight, then you have fatty liver and you may develop more serious complications.

Fatty liver may cause no damage, but sometimes the excess fat leads to inflammation of the liver. This condition, called steatohepatitis, does cause liver damage. Sometimes, inflammation from a fatty liver is linked to alcohol abuse. This is known as alcoholic steatohepatitis. Otherwise, the condition is called non-alcoholic steatohepatitis, or NASH.

An inflamed liver may become scarred and hardened over time. This condition, called cirrhosis, is serious and often leads to liver failure.NASH is one of the top three leading causes of cirrhosis.

## Causes

Eating excess calories causes fat to build up in the liver. When the liver does not process and break down fats as it normally should, too much fat will accumulate. People tend to develop fatty liver if they have certain other conditions, such as obesity, diabetes or high triglycerides.

Alcohol abuse, rapid weight loss and malnutrition may also lead to fatty liver.However, some people develop fatty liver even if they have none of these conditions.

## Risk Factors

Most, but not all fatty liver patients are middle-aged and overweight. The risk factors most commonly linked to fatty liver disease are:

- Overweight (body mass index of 25-30)
- Obesity (body mass index above 30)
- Diabetes
- Elevated triglyceride levels.

## Metabolic Syndrome And Fatty Liver Disease

Many researchers now believe that metabolic syndrome – a cluster of disorders that increase the risk of diabetes, heart disease and stroke – plays an important role in the development of fatty liver.

Signs and symptoms of metabolic syndrome include:

- Obesity, particularly around the waist (abdominal obesity)
- High blood pressure (hypertension)
- One or more abnormal cholesterol levels — high levels of triglycerides, a type of blood fat, or low levels of high-density lipoprotein (hdl) cholesterol, the 'good' cholesterol
- Resistance to insulin, a hormone that helps to regulate the amount of sugar in the blood.

Of these, insulin resistance may be the most important trigger of NASH. Because the condition can remain stable for many years, causing little harm, researchers have proposed that a 'second hit' to the liver, such as a bacterial infection or hormonal abnormality, may lead to cirrhosis.

## How A Liver Becomes Fatty

It is unclear how a liver becomes fatty. The fat may come from other parts of your body, or your liver may absorb an increased amount of fat from your intestine. Another possible explanation is that the liver loses its ability to change fat into a form that can be eliminated. However, the eating of fatty foods, by itself, doesn't produce a fatty liver.

## Symptoms Of Fatty Liver Disease

A fatty liver produces no symptoms on its own, so people often learn about their fatty liver when they have medical tests for other reasons. NASH can damage your liver for years or even decades without causing any symptoms. If the disease gets worse, you may experience fatigue, weight loss, abdominal discomfort, weakness and confusion.

## Diagnosis Of Fatty Liver Disease

Your doctor may see something unusual in a blood test or notice that your liver is slightly enlarged during a routine check-up. These could be signs of a fatty liver. To make sure you don't have another liver disease, your doctor may ask for more blood tests (including liver function tests), an ultrasound, a computed tomography (CT) scan or medical resonance imaging (an MRI).

If other diseases are ruled out, you may be diagnosed with NASH. The only way to know for sure is to get a liver biopsy. Your doctor will remove a sample of liver tissue with a needle and check it under a microscope.

Some questions to ask your doctor after diagnosis include:

- What is the likely cause of my fatty liver?
- Do I have NASH? If not, how likely am I to develop NASH?
- Do I have cirrhosis? If not, how likely am I to develop cirrhosis?
- Do I need to lose weight? How can I do so safely?
- Should I be taking any medication to control my cholesterol and triglyceride levels?
- What medications or other substances should I avoid to protect my liver?

## Prevention And Reversal Of Fatty Liver Disease

There are no medical or surgical treatments for fatty liver, but some steps may help prevent or reverse some of the damage.

In general, if you have fatty liver, and in particular if you have NASH, you should:

- Lose weight – safely. This usually means losing no more than half to one kilogram (one to two pounds) a week

- lower your triglycerides through diet, medication or both

- avoid alcohol

- control your diabetes, if you have it

- eat a balanced, healthy diet

- increase your physical activity

- get regular check-ups from a doctor who specialises in liver care.

## Treatment

Fatty liver is currently the focus of intense research. Scientists are studying whether various medications can help reduce liver inflammation, including new diabetes medications that may help you even if you don't have diabetes. These include metformin, pioglitazone, rosiglitazone and betaine.Another drug being investigated is orlistat (Xenical), a medication that blocks the absorption of some of the fat from your food. Early results indicate that orlistat may reduce the amount of fat in the liver.

## Foods To Help Fatty Liver Reversal

Treating fatty liver disease with food

There are two major types of fatty liver disease — alcohol-induced and nonalcoholic fatty liver disease. Fatty liver disease affects nearly one-third of American adults and is one of the leading contributors to liver failure. Nonalcoholic fatty liver disease is most commonly diagnosed in those who are obese or sedentary and those who eat a highly processed diet.

One of the main ways to treat fatty liver disease, regardless of type, is with diet. As the name suggests, fatty liver disease means you have too much fat in your liver. In a healthy body, the liver helps to remove toxins and produces bile, the digestive protein. Fatty liver disease damages the liver and prevents it from working as well as it should.

In general, the diet for fatty liver disease includes:

- Lots of fruits and vegetables
- High-fiber plants like legumes and whole grains
- Very little added sugar, salt, trans fat, refined carbohydrates, and saturated fat
- No alcohol

A low-fat, reduced-calorie diet can help you lose weight and reduce the risk of fatty liver disease. Ideally, if you're overweight, you would aim to lose at least 10 percent of your body weight.

## Foods And Drinks That You Should Eat For A Fatty Liver

Here are a few foods to include in your healthy liver diet:

1. Coffee to lower abnormal liver enzymes

Studies have shown that coffee drinkers with fatty liver disease have less liver damage than those who don't drink this caffeinated beverage. Caffeine appears to lower the amount of abnormal liver enzymes of people at risk for liver diseases.

2. Greens to prevent fat buildup

Broccoli is shown to help prevent the buildup of fat in the liverTrusted Source in mice. Eating more greens, like spinach, Brussels sprouts, and kale, can also help with general weight loss. Try the Canadian Liver Foundation's recipe for vegetarian chili, which lets you cut back on calories without sacrificing flavor.

3. Tofu to reduce fat buildup

A University of Illinois study on rats found that soy protein, which is contained in foods like tofu, may reduce fat buildup in the liver. Plus, tofu is low in fat and high in protein.

4. Fish for inflammation and fat levels

Fatty fish such as salmon, sardines, tuna, and trout are high in omega-3 fatty acids. Omega-3 fatty acids can help improve liver fat levelsTrusted Source and bring down inflammationTrusted Source. Try this teriyaki halibut recipe, recommended by the Canadian Liver Foundation, that's especially low in fat.

5. Oatmeal for energy

Carbohydrates from whole grains like oatmeal give your body energy. Their fiber content also fills you up, which can help you maintain your weight.

6. Walnuts to improve the liver

These nuts are high in omega-3 fatty acids. Research findsTrusted Source that people with fatty liver disease who eat walnuts have improved liver function tests.

7. Avocado to help protect the liver

Avocados are high in healthy fats, and research suggests they contain chemicals that might slow liver damage. They're also rich in fiber, which can help with weight control. Try this refreshing avocado and mushroom salad from Fatty Liver Diet Review.

8. Milk and other low-fat dairy to protect from damage

Dairy is high in whey protein, which may protect the liver from further damage, according to a 2011 studyTrusted Source in rats.

9. Sunflower seeds for antioxidants

These nutty-tasting seeds are high in vitamin E, an antioxidant that may protect the liver from further damage.

10. Olive oil for weight control

This healthy oil is high in omega-3 fatty acids. It's healthier for cooking than margarine, butter, or shortening. ResearchTrusted Source finds that olive oil helps to lower liver enzyme levels and control weight. Try this liver-friendly take on a traditional Mexican dish from LiverSupport.com.

11. Garlic to help reduce body weight

This herb not only adds flavor to food, but experimental studies also show that garlic powder supplementsTrusted Source may help reduce body weight and fat in people with fatty liver disease.

12. Green tea for less fat absorption

Data supports that green tea can help interfere with fat absorption, but the results aren't conclusive yet. Researchers are studying whether green tea can reduce fat storage in the liver and improve liver function. But green tea also has many benefits, from lowering cholesterol to aiding with sleep.

## Foods To Avoid If You Have A Fatty Liver

There are definitely foods you should avoid or limit if you have fatty liver disease. These foods generally contribute to weight gain and increasing blood sugar.

Avoid

Alcohol. Alcohol is a major cause of fatty liver disease as well as other liver diseases.

Added sugar. Stay away from sugary foods such as candy, cookies, sodas, and fruit juices. High blood sugar increases the amount of fat buildup in the liver.

Fried foods. These are high in fat and calories.

Salt. Eating too much salt can make your body hold on to excess water. Limit sodium to less than 1,500 milligrams per day.

White bread, rice, and pasta. White usually means the flour is highly processed, which can raise your blood sugar more than whole grains due to a lack of fiber.

Red meat. Beef and deli meats are high in saturated fat.

## What Does A Diet Plan Look Like?

Here's what your menu might look like during a typical day on a fatty liver diet plan:

Meal

breakfast

• 8 oz. hot oatmeal mixed with 2 tsp. almond butter and 1 sliced banana

• 1 cup coffee with low-fat or skim milk

lunch

• spinach salad with balsamic vinegar and olive oil dressing

- 3 oz. grilled chicken

- 1 small baked potato

- 1 cup cooked broccoli, carrots, or other vegetable

- 1 apple

- 1 glass of milk

snack •

1 tbsp. peanut butter on sliced apples or 2 tbsp. hummus with raw veggies

dinner •

small mixed-bean salad

- 3 oz. grilled salmon

- 1 cup cooked broccoli

- 1 whole-grain roll

- 1 cup mixed berries

- 1 glass of milk

In addition to modifying your diet, here are a few other lifestyle changes you can make to improve your liver health:

Get more active. Exercise, paired with diet, can help you lose extra weight and manage your liver disease. Aim to get at least 30 minutes of aerobic exercise on most days of the week.

Lower cholesterol. Watch your saturated fat and sugar intake to help keep your cholesterol and triglyceride levels under control. If diet and exercise aren't enough to lower your cholesterol, ask your doctor about taking medication.

Control diabetes. Diabetes and fatty liver disease often occur together. Diet and exercise can help you manage both conditions. If your blood sugar is still high, your doctor can prescribe medication to lower it.

# Recipes

Liver & mash

Ingredients

For the mash

3 large baking potatoes

½ tsp olive oil

150ml whole milk

1 tbsp butter

pinch of freshly grated nutmeg

For the herb butter

100g butter, softened

½ tbsp chopped parsley

For the liver

1 tbsp plain flour

200g lamb's liver, trimmed and cut into 2 pieces (approx 1cm thick)

1-2 tbsp sunflower oil

small handful of mini silverskin pickled onions

2 garlic cloves, very finely chopped

Method

Heat oven to 200C/180C/gas 6. Prick the potatoes all over with a fork, rub with oil and bake directly on the oven shelf for 1 hr 20 mins. Once cooked, leave for 10-15 mins or until cool enough to handle, then slice in half, scoop out the potato flesh and push it through a potato ricer or colander. Cover until needed. (I like to keep the potato skins for another day and stuff them with leftover mash, softened leeks and cheese, and bake until golden and bubbling.)

Mix the herb butter ingredients together, spread out into a rough log shape on a piece of baking parchment, roll up and twist the ends tightly so it resembles a cracker. Put in the freezer for 10-15 mins to firm up.

Heat the milk and butter for the mash in a saucepan until the butter has melted and the mixture starts to simmer. Pour this over the potato flesh, mash it and sprinkle over the nutmeg and some seasoning. Keep warm or reheat when serving.

Heat a large, non-stick pan over a medium-high heat. Season the flour with pepper, then use it to very lightly dust the liver. Pour the oil into the hot pan, season the liver well with sea salt, then fry for no more than 2 mins each side. Transfer to a plate and cover with foil.

Turn down the heat, but while the oil's still hot, add the pickled onions. As the onions start to caramelise, put them on the plate with the liver. Add the garlic to the pan, which by now should be sufficiently cooled enough not to burn it. Add a little oil to the pan if it looks dry. Once the garlic is starting to soften but not coloured at all, add 4-5 thin slices of the parsley butter and some of the resting juices from the liver plate. Turn off the heat and allow the butter to melt but not colour.

Heap your mash onto two plates, top with the liver, sliced if you like, and the onions. Then generously drizzle over the herb butter. Serve with a crisp, mustardy salad.

## Liver & bacon with onion gravy

Ingredients

4 rashers smoked streaky bacon

2 tbsp plain flour, seasoned

pinch dried sage

(optional)

6 slices lamb's livers (about 400g/14oz)

1 tbsp olive oil

1 onion, thinly sliced

300ml beef stock

2 tbsp ketchup

Method

Cook the bacon in a large non-stick frying pan until crisp. Meanwhile, mix the flour and sage, if using, and use to dust the liver. Remove bacon from the pan and set aside. Add the oil to the pan and brown the liver for about 1 min on each side. Remove from the pan, then fry the onion until softened. Stir in stock and ketchup, then bubble for 5 mins.

Put the liver back in the pan and cook for 3 mins until cooked through. Serve with the bacon broken over the top and some mash. (see related recipes)

## Faux gras with toast & pickles

Ingredients

100g butter, softened

300g organic chicken or duck livers, trimmed, cleaned and patted dry

To serve

sliced brioche or sourdough

cornichons

chutney

sea salt flakes

Method

Heat 50g butter in a frying pan until sizzling, add the livers and fry for 4 mins until coloured on the outside and slightly pink in the middle. Leave to cool, then tip the contents of the pan into a food processor or a smoothie bullet blender. Season generously with salt and add the remaining butter. Blitz until you have a smooth purée, then scrape into a container, smooth over the top and place in the fridge to chill for at least 2 hrs. Can be made a day ahead.

To serve, griddle slices of brioche or sourdough, and tip some cornichons and chutney into small pots. Put a large spoon in a cup of hot water. As if serving ice cream, scoop a spoonful of the faux gras onto each plate, dipping the spoon into the water after each scoop. Sprinkle a few salt flakes over each scoop and serve with the toasts, cornichons and chutney.

## Liver & bacon sauté with potatoes & parsley

Ingredients

400g new potato

2 tbsp olive oil

4 spring onions, trimmed and each cut into 2-3 pieces on the diagonal

4 rashers of unsmoked bacon, snipped into pieces

1 tbsp plain flour

1 tsp paprika, plus extra for sprinkling

175g lamb's liver, sliced into thin strips

20g pack flatleaf parsley, chopped

150ml hot vegetable stock (made with bouillon powder)

4 tbsp soured cream

Method

Halve the potatoes. Simmer in salted water for 12-15 minutes. Drain and set aside.

Heat the oil in a wok. Add the potatoes and fry them for 4-5 minutes over a high heat until browned and crispy. Remove from the pan and set aside.

Tip the spring onions and bacon into the pan and stir and sizzle for 3-4 minutes or until the bacon gets crispy. Meanwhile, season the flour with paprika, a little salt and plenty of black pepper, then use to coat the liver.

Stir the liver into the pan and cook for 2-3 minutes. Toss in the potatoes and quickly reheat. Stir in the chopped parsley, remove everything from the pan and divide between 2 plates. Keep warm.

Quickly pour the hot stock into the pan and scrape all the crispy bits up from the bottom. Bubble for 1-2 minutes, then pour around the liver and potatoes. Serve each portion topped with soured cream and a sprinkling of paprika.

## Chicken livers on toast

Ingredients

250g chicken livers

2 shallots, finely chopped

large handful flatleaf parsley, leaves very roughly chopped

1 tbsp capers, rinsed and drained, roughly chopped

2 tbsp olive oil

3 tbsp sherry vinegar

4 slices nice bread, such as sourdough

1 tbsp plain flour

large pinch cayenne pepper

Method

Pick over the livers, cutting away any fatty bits and sinew, then pat the livers dry. Place the shallot, parsley and capers into a bowl and drizzle with half the olive oil and 1 tbsp of the Sherry vinegar.

Toast the bread (preferably on a griddle but a toaster is fine). Toss the livers in the flour and cayenne pepper, and season generously with salt and pepper. Heat the rest of the oil in a frying pan and fry the livers over a really high heat for 4-5 mins until brown and crisp on the outside and cooked, but still a little pink in the middle. Splash remaining vinegar into the pan and bubble down for 1 min.

Tip the contents of the pan in with the shallot and parsley, toss everything together, season to taste, then pile onto the toasted bread. Season with a little crunchy sea salt and serve.



Ingredients

25g butter

1 shallot, finely chopped

2 garlic cloves, 1 crushed, 1 squashed

200g chorizo, skin removed, sliced

4 thick slices of bread

1 tbsp olive oil, plus extra for drizzling (optional)

300g chicken liver, trimmed of any sinew or tubes

good splash of dry sherry (Fino works well)

4 tbsp double cream

small handful of parsley, chopped

Method

Melt the butter in a frying pan. When sizzling, add the shallot and the crushed garlic, and stir around the pan for 1-2 mins to soften. Add the chorizo and cook for 4 mins over a medium heat to release some of the oils.

Meanwhile, heat a griddle pan until hot. Drizzle the slices of bread with the olive oil and rub the squashed garlic all over the surface. Put on the griddle pan and cook for 1 min each side until nicely charred with lines.

Turn up the heat under the chorizo pan, add the chicken livers and sear for 1 min. Add the sherry, bubble for 1 min more, add the cream and parsley, then season well. Put 2 slices of bread on each plate, top with the chicken liver mixture and a drizzle of oil, if you like.

## Chicken liver & chorizo salad

Ingredients

200g cooking chorizo, cut into chunks

25g butter

350g good chicken livers, cleaned and trimmed

110g bag baby salad leaves

bunch parsley, roughly chopped

large handful walnut

halves

For the dressing

1 tbsp walnut oil

1 tbsp white wine vinegar

Method

Cook the chorizo in a large frying pan until crisp. Remove with a slotted spoon and set aside, reserving 1 tbsp of the chorizo oil. For the dressing, whisk together the walnut oil, reserved chorizo oil and white wine vinegar, then season.

Melt the butter in the same pan until sizzling, then cook the chicken livers for about 2 mins each side. Combine everything together in a large bowl, then drizzle over the dressing, toss well and serve straight away

## Chicken liver & mushroom nests

Ingredients

3 tbsp sunflower oil

3 onions, finely chopped

250g pack chestnut mushroom, chopped

1 garlic clove, crushed

400g pack chicken liver, trimmed of any sinewy bits

3 tbsp brandy

140g white breadcrumb

bunch flatleaf parsley, chopped

handful walnuts, chopped

12 smoked, dry-cured streaky bacon rashers

Method

Heat oven to 190C/170C fan/gas 5. Heat the oil in a large frying pan, then soften the onions for 10 mins with the pan covered. Turn up the heat, add the mushrooms and fry for about 10 mins until golden and all their liquid has evaporated. Stir in the garlic and cook for 1 min more. Tip everything onto a plate.

Pat the livers dry, then add a little more oil to the pan. Sizzle in batches for about 20 secs on each side until just golden but not cooked through. Set aside on a plate as you go. Tip in the brandy and let it reduce to 1 tbsp. Roughly chop the livers once cooled, then mix with the oniony mushrooms, brandy, bread and almost all the parsley and nuts.

To cook, wind bacon rashers into the wells of a 12-hole bun tin, like little nests. Spoon in the stuffing (reserving 250g for your turkey), scatter with remaining nuts, then bake, covered with foil, for 20 mins. Uncover and cook for 25 mins more until the bacon is gold. Scatter with remaining chopped parsley to serve.

## Calves' liver with sticky onion relish & prosciutto

Ingredients

250g calves' liver, sliced

a little olive oil

2 slices prosciutto

1 tbsp flour, seasoned

small handful sage leaves

150ml marsala or madeira

knob of butter

seasonal greens, to serve (optional)

potatoes, to serve (optional)

For the onion relish

600g (3 large) red onions, very thinly sliced

6 juniper berries, lightly crushed

leaves from a few thyme sprigs

100ml red wine vinegar

5 tbsp light muscovado sugar

Method

To make the relish, put the onions, juniper and thyme in a large saucepan, season with 1 tsp salt and a little pepper. Cook on a high heat for 10 mins, stirring regularly as the onions start to soften. Add the vinegar, sugar and 100ml water. Cover, boil for 5 mins, then uncover and simmer gently for 5 mins or until soft and with a little juice remaining. Meanwhile, remove large tubes, membrane or gristle from the liver. Pat dry with kitchen paper.

Heat 1 tsp oil in a large frying pan and add the prosciutto. Fry for 1 min each side or until golden and crisp. Set aside on a plate and keep warm in a low oven.

Add a splash more oil to the pan. Dust the liver slices in the flour and pat away any excess. Place the liver in the hot pan, scatter the sage in, then fry for 1 min each side if the liver is sliced thinly, longer if thicker. When the liver is golden and just pink in the middle, transfer it and the crisped sage to the plate in the oven.

Return the pan to the hob and add the Marsala. Boil until syrupy. Let the butter melt into this sauce, season to taste, then set aside. If your sauce reduces too quickly, just add a little water. Plate up the liver, prosciutto, sage and warm onion relish, then spoon over the sauce. Serve with seasonal greens and potatoes, if you like.

## Liver with wild mushrooms

Ingredients

3 tbsp dripping or lard

500-600g/1lb 2oz-1lb 5oz lobe of free-range pork liver - ask your butcher for a thick piece

1 shallot, finely choppd

For the mushroom ragout

500g mixed fresh wild mushroom - Horn of Plenty or Penny Buns (ceps) are best

3 tbsp olive oil or butter

1 large onion, finely chopped

1 garlic clove, finely sliced

1 thyme

sprig

2 sage

leaves, chopped

2 tbsp dry sherry

50ml dry white wine

250ml chicken stock

100ml double cream

Method

Heat oven to 200C/180C fan/gas 6. Place a large frying pan over a high heat and, when hot, add the dripping or lard. When it's melted, add the liver. Let the liver brown well on each side, sprinkling it with some seasoning as it cooks.

When the liver is browned, transfer it to a roasting tin. Sprinkle it with the shallot and put it in the oven for 20-25 mins. When the liver is firm to the touch, or registers 55C on an electric cooking thermometer in its thickest part, remove it from the oven and set it to rest in a warm place, lightly covered.

While the liver cooks, prepare the mushrooms. Brush them to remove any grit or soil. Place a large saucepan over a medium-high heat and add the olive oil or butter. Cook the mushrooms with a little seasoning so that they brown a little and all the liquid evaporates. Add the onion and garlic to the pan and reduce the heat to medium. Continue to cook until the mushrooms begin to soften, then add the thyme and sage. Stir together well, then add the Sherry and white wine.

Turn the heat to high and boil the juices so that they reduce by half. Add the stock and repeat. When the juices in the pan are reduced and slightly thickened, add the cream and stir to combine. Taste the juices and correct the seasoning if required.

When the liver has rested, slice it thinly and serve immediately, topped with the mushroom ragout, on warm plates.

Ingredients

8 slices pancetta

(or streaky bacon)

1 tbsp vegetable oil

500g calves' liver, sliced into 4 steaks

50g butter

small bunch sage, leaves picked, most roughly chopped

½ small bunch thyme, leaves picked

4 shallots, finely sliced

300g mixed wild or chestnut mushroom, cleaned

zest and juice ½ lemon

4 thick slices of rustic bread, toasted (preferably sourdough)

Method

Put the pancetta in a large frying pan and cook until crisp, then lift out with a slotted spoon and drain on kitchen paper. Heat the oil in the pan. Sear the liver steaks for 1-2 mins each side – so they're just still pink in the middle – using half the butter towards the end to baste the meat. Remove the liver to a plate using the slotted spoon and leave to rest, covered with foil, for 10-15 mins.

Add the chopped sage, thyme leaves, shallots, mushrooms and lemon zest to the pan. Fry on the highest heat for a few mins, then add the lemon juice and some seasoning. Cook for 3-5 mins until slightly saucy and the mushrooms are soft.

Heat the remaining butter in your smallest saucepan until just foaming. Add the remaining whole sage leaves and fry for a few mins until crisp. Drain on kitchen paper with the pancetta. Sit the liver on toast, spoon over the mushroom mixture and scatter over the pancetta and crisp sage. Serve immediately.

## Liver parfait with Sauternes jelly

Ingredients

200g unsalted butter

3 banana shallots, finely chopped

1 bay leaf

3 thyme sprigs

500g chicken livers (see tip, below left, for how to prepare)

100ml Sauternes

100ml double cream

3 medium eggs, at room temperature

brioche or bread, toasted (or gluten free alternative), to serve

cornichons, to serve

For the jelly

3 sheets leaf gelatine

250ml Sauternes

50g golden caster sugar

a few thyme leaves (optional)

Method

Melt the butter in a wide frying pan and add the shallots, herbs and some seasoning. Cook gently for 10 mins until very soft.

Spoon the shallots into a food processor and discard the herbs; pour the butter into a jug, leaving 1 tbsp in the pan.

Turn up the heat in the pan and add the livers. Season and fry for 30 secs on each side or until just browned all over. They will still be very raw inside. Take out of the pan and put in the processor. Splash the Sauternes into the hot pan and reduce by half, scraping up any tasty bits as it bubbles. Tip onto the liver and shallots.

Process the livers until totally smooth. With the motor running, slowly pour in the cream and add the eggs, one by one, then the warm butter. Season with 2 tsp sea salt and some pepper, but don't taste the mixture as it's still raw. Pass through a sieve, using a spatula to help.

Heat oven to 160C/140C fan/gas 3 and boil a full kettle. Put 6 heatproof glass tumblers, small Kilner jars or large ramekins into a roasting tin. Pour the parfait into each one. Pour hot water around the parfaits, letting it come as far up the sides as is safe for you to carry. Bake for 45 mins until the parfaits have set without a wobble and risen a little in the middle. Cool at room temperature (I make this more speedy by filling the pan with cold water and letting the whole thing stand on a wire rack), then chill.

To make the jelly, soak the gelatine in cold water until it is totally floppy. Heat the wine and sugar until it dissolves, then remove from the heat. Squeeze out as much water from the gelatine as possible, then stir into the wine until totally dissolved. Set aside. When cooled but still liquid, pour this over the top of the parfaits, adding a few thyme leaves here and there. Leave to set in the fridge for at least 30 mins. Can be made up to 2 days ahead. Serve with toast and cornichons.

## Sautéed liver & apple salad with blackberry dressing

Ingredients

2 tbsp butter

3 sharp eating apples, such as Braeburn, peeled and cut into sugar-cube-sized pieces

500g chicken livers, trimmed (see tip, below left, for how to prepare)

3 tbsp plain flour, seasoned generously

100g bag salad leaves

100g walnut halves, toasted

crusty bread, to serve (optional)

For the dressing

200g blackberries

smart tart berries are better than dessert ones

2 tbsp red wine or Port

2 tbsp balsamic vinegar

2 tbsp golden caster sugar, plus extra if needed

2 tsp extra virgin olive oil

Method

Make the dressing first. Set aside 8 of the berries in a bowl. Put the rest of the berries, the wine, vinegar and sugar in a medium pan, cover and simmer for 3 mins or until the berries are very soft. Mash the berries well, then pass the hot mixture though a sieve, on top of the reserved berries. Season and cool. It should be quite sharp and fruity, but blackberries vary hugely; if you need to, add more sugar and taste again.

Heat 1 tbsp butter in a large non-stick frying pan and add the apples. Cook for about 5 mins, turning the apples now and again, until golden and just tender. Can be done a few hours ahead.

When you're ready to eat, dredge the livers in the seasoned flour and tap off the excess. Heat the rest of the butter in the pan and fry the livers for 5 mins or until golden, turning them halfway through cooking. When red juices start to run from the livers, you know that they are almost ready. Toss the apples back in the pan to warm through, then take it off the heat.

Spread the salad leaves across 1 large platter or 4 plates, and top with the livers, apples and walnuts. Whisk the oil into the blackberry dressing and spoon this over generously. Serve with crusty bread, if you like.

## Chicken liver pâté

Ingredients

375g unsalted butter

400g chicken livers, trimmed

2 large garlic cloves, 1 crushed, 1 finely sliced

3 thyme sprigs, leaves only

3 tbsp madeira

4 slices brioche

1 Bramley apple, cored and diced

onion chutney, to serve

cornichons, to serve

Method

Heat 1 tbsp of the butter in a non-stick frying pan over a medium heat. When the butter is foaming, add the chicken livers and fry for 2 mins each side.

Stir the crushed garlic, some of the thyme and Madeira into the pan with the livers. Fry for 2 mins, letting the Madeira simmer. Transfer the mixture to a food processor, reserve 200g of the butter and add the rest to the processor. Blend everything to a smooth paste. Season to taste, then spoon into 4 x 70ml clip-top jars.

Melt the reserved butter in a medium frying pan and add the sliced garlic. Turn the garlic in the butter until slightly golden. Pour into the 4 jars of pâté, ensuring a few slices of garlic and the remaining thyme leaves go in each jar, and chill in the fridge for at least 4 hrs, or until set. Can be made up to 2 days in advance.

Before serving, toast the brioche, then cut into triangular quarters for serving. Stir the diced apple through the chutney. Serve the pâté on small wooden boards with the toasted brioche, cornichons and chutney.

## Chicken liver & pineau pâté

Ingredients

500g chicken livers

100g butter

100g unsmoked lardons or chopped streaky bacon

1 garlic clove, crushed or finely chopped

1 tbsp fresh thyme

leaves or 1 tsp dried

5 tbsp pineau or sherry

herb sprigs to garnish, rosemary, thyme or bay

toasted brioche or raisin bread and cornichons, to serve

Method

Rinse the chicken livers and cut away any dark patches and small stringy threads. Pat dry with kitchen paper. Heat 25g of the butter in a frying pan until foaming, then add the lardons or bacon and fry until crisp. Add the garlic, chicken livers and thyme and fry briskly for about 5 mins, until they are evenly browned. They should be nicely browned on the outside, but pink inside and should feel squashy when pressed.

Add the pineau, salt and pepper, then bubble for a few mins. Remove from the heat. Blitz the mixture in a food processor until smooth, then spoon into a jar or dish. Smooth the top.

Melt the remaining butter, put a herb sprig or bay leaf on top of the pâté and pour over the butter, leaving the sediment behind. Leave to cool, then chill until set.4 Serve spooned from the dish with toasted brioche, a bowl of cornichons and a little sea salt.

## Faggots with onion gravy

Ingredients

little oil, for the tin

170g pack sage & onion stuffing mix (we used Paxo)

500g pack diced pork shoulder

300g pig liver

½ tsp ground mace

For the gravy

2 onions, thinly sliced

1 tbsp sunflower oil

2 tsp sugar

1 tbsp red wine vinegar

3 tbsp plain flour

850ml beef stock

handful chopped parsley

mash and veg, to serve (optional)

Method

Heat oven to 160C/140C fan/gas 3. Lightly oil a very large roasting tin. Tip the stuffing mix into a large bowl, add 500ml boiling water, stir and set aside.

Pulse the pork in a food processor until finely chopped. Add the liver and pulse again. Add to the stuffing with the mace, 1 tsp salt and plenty of black pepper. Stir well. Shape the mixture (it will be very soft) into 24 large faggots and put in the prepared tin.

To make the gravy, fry the onions in the oil until starting to turn golden. Add the sugar and continue cooking, stirring frequently, until caramelised. Tip in the vinegar and allow to sizzle. Mix the flour with a couple of tbsp water. Pour the stock into the onions, then add the flour paste and cook, stirring constantly, until smooth and starting to thicken. When it is thick, pour into the tin with the faggots, cover with foil and bake for 1 hr until cooked through. Serve sprinkled with parsley, with mash and a veg, if you like.

## Country terrine with black pepper & thyme

Ingredients

butter, for greasing

750g streaky pork

rashers

1 tbsp dried thyme

1 tsp black peppercorns

2 x 225g tubs frozen chicken livers, thawed

4 tbsp red or white wine (optional)

5 rashers smoked streaky bacon

cocktail gherkins or chutney, to serve

Method

Heat oven to 180C/fan 160C/gas 4 and butter a 1kg loaf tin. Roughly chop 3 of the pork rashers and mix with the thyme and peppercorns. Set aside. Put the remaining pork rashers into a food processor with two-thirds of the chicken livers, the wine (if using) and 1 tsp salt, then blend to make a smooth pâté.

Spoon half the pâté into the loaf tin, then top with the chopped pork mixture and remaining livers. Spoon the rest of the pâté mixture over the livers, then lay the 5 smoked bacon rashers lengthwise over the top.

Cover the loaf tin with foil and put in a roasting tin. Pour cold water into the roasting tin until it is half-filled, then bake for 1½ hrs until the terrine is set. When the terrine is cool, put another loaf tin on top and weigh it down (with cans from your storecupboard) to compress it. Leave overnight in the fridge. Can be made and chilled up to 2 days ahead.

To serve, turn the terrine out of the tin and carefully cut into slices with a sharp knife. Serve with the French toasts (recipe below) and cocktail gherkins or chutney.

## Poule au pot with stuffing balls & garlic cream

Ingredients

1½ kg chicken

300ml white wine

1 onion, peeled but left whole

3 cloves

1 bouquet garni (tied bundle of herbs)

2 garlic cloves

12 small potatoes

4 carrots, cut into 5cm lengths

2 turnips, cut into wedges

3 leeks, cut into 5cm lengths

roughly chopped parsley, to serve

For the stuffing balls

200g lean minced pork

100g streaky bacon, cut into dice

100g chicken livers, finely chopped

2 tbsp olive oil

2 shallots, diced

2 garlic cloves, crushed

1 egg, beaten

handful parsley

leaves, chopped

100g fresh white breadcrumbs

For the garlic cream

3 garlic cloves, left whole

200ml tub crème fraîche

Method

Heat oven to 180C/160C fan/gas 4. Put the chicken in a flameproof casserole dish and pour over 600ml water and the wine. Stud the onion with the cloves. Add to the pan with the bouquet garni, garlic and seasoning, then bring to the boil. Cover and put in the oven for 1½ hrs.

To make the garlic cream, simmer the unpeeled garlic cloves in a small pan of water for 30 mins until soft. When cool enough to handle, squeeze out into a bowl and mash with salt and pepper. Stir in the crème fraîche and tip into a bowl, then keep in the fridge until needed.

For the stuffing, mix the meats in a bowl. Heat the oil in a small pan and gently fry the shallots and garlic until softened but not browned. Add to the bowl with the egg, parsley, breadcrumbs, seasoning, then mix well. Shape into 18 balls and put in a shallow baking tray.

Remove chicken after 1½ hrs and put it on the hob on medium heat. Place the stuffing in the oven for 25-30 mins until browned and crisp. Add the vegetables to the chicken pot. Cook for 25-30 mins, then lift out the chicken to a plate and keep the veg warm in the stock.

Remove chicken's skin, and break the flesh into chunks. Put on a warm platter with the stuffing and the veg. Add a ladle of cooking stock and the parsley.Serve the rest of the cooking juices in a jug.

## Conclusion

There are currently no drugs on the market that are approved by the U.S. Food and Drug Administration for fatty liver disease. While losing 10 percent of your weight is ideal, even just 3 to 5 percent can help. Ask your doctor to check your blood for the hepatitis A and B vaccines as well.These can help prevent viruses from causing liver damage.